NAKA

POEMS
FROM
THE
CENTER

ROLLAND G. SMITH

NAKA

POEMS
FROM
THE
CENTER

ROLLAND G. SMITH

Smith, Rolland G., 1941–
    Naka: Poetry/Rolland G. Smith

ISBN 978-0-9920920-4-7

Satellight Producers Corporation
www.rollandgsmith.com

Editing: Angela Wingfield, Fine Tune Communications
Cover and layout design: Ellen Mann, Kemias Enterprises
Photography: Claude Charlebois, Sheila Ryan DeBold, Ellen Mann,
                Rolland Smith
Illustration "Sir Winston": Ed Berkise

Printed in the United States

Dedication

Shortly before my wife died, she was reading a book on Henry David Thoreau's writings. She said to me, "If I could write the preface for your next poetry book, I would write what I just read, for it is you."

She handed me the book and pointed to the passage. It comes from Thoreau's journal.

> The thinker, he who is serene and self-possessed . . . He who can deal with his thoughts as a material, building them into poems in which future generations will delight, he is the man of the greatest and rarest vigor. . . . He is a man of energy, in whom settled and poetic thoughts are bred. . . . There is no more Herculean task than to think a thought about this life and then get it expressed.

Thank you, Ann Gormley Smith. Requiescat in pace.

Poetry is the spontaneous overflow of powerful
feelings recollected in moments of tranquillity.

—William Wordsworth

Contents

Preface

There are many Western poetic schools. In this tome you will find a smattering of styles, but my passion is rhyme and syllabic meter as well as sound. I would encourage all readers to recite poetry out loud. Sound is the pigment of poetry. It gives color to metaphor, luster to allegory and awareness to meaning.

Because I retain a journalistic curiosity, I invite you to email your comments, likes or dislikes, on selected or collective poems presented in this book to rollandgsmith@mac.com.

Special Thanks

A profound thank-you goes to my long-time friend Ellen Mann. Without her encouragement, enthusiasm, nudging and gentle reminders *Naka* would still be in folders on my computer.

Ellen is the producer of many creative works of the word. Poets and writers have relied on her expertise to bring thought to form and to bring spirit to the printed page. She was instrumental in the formation of my first three books: *Quiet Musings*, *Encore*, and *Stone Wisdom*.

I give her eternal hugs of appreciation for being the catalyst of creativity and a friend from the spiritual cluster of Being.

One Leaves First

Oh, how I wish it were not so
To live within an empty house
That once was whole, so short ago
Before the passing of my spouse.

Beyond the pain of letting go
And tossing stuff and learning chores,
There are the memories that I know
When finding things in bureau drawers.

I found a card that I once wrote.
She saved it with some other things,
Photographs and an old school note,
Some trinkets too and grandma's rings.

Fifty years, plus another two,
We had together living life.
A century half and more, too few
When looking back as man and wife.

I talk to her most all the time.
I know my ears can't hear her voice,
But there's a sense of love sublime,
And mending thoughts provide a choice.

As she is there and I am here
With only inches in-between.
The spirit states there is no fear
For life exists past earthly dream.

The hardest thing it seems to me
Is living new when life's reversed.
The saddest thing I know to be
Was knowing that she'd go home first.

Illusion's Truth

I felt the wind and saw the clouds
And I'm delighted in the scene,
For there I saw all human crowds
Betwixt, bewildered, in between.

When all is up and nothing's down,
There comes a time to let it go,
For past the line are times of clowns
As ego's magic bides its glow.

But in the clouds and swirling wind
There is a key to comprehend.
That life is choice we can't rescind
To learn and grow and then transcend.

If dogma's greed does stop your quest
And hold you from your inner truth
And keep you silent in the breast,
Perhaps you need an auger's sooth.

THE TEAHOUSE OF THE SUMMER SUN

Beyond the thought of standing still
And wondering what's held within,
Perhaps the light of heaven's grace
Allows the prayerful to begin.

Young trees stand sentry to this place
To grace love's presence everywhere
Especially in sacred times
When setting sun releases care.

The teahouse is a special place
For souls who've gone and those who stay.
It blends beneath its raftered roof
A place to think and one to pray.

The Voice

I heard a voice the other day.
It simply said, "I love my trees."
The sky had clouds in swirled gray
With beams of light that bent my knees.

I listened more to what was said:
"My trees are friends and teachers too.
They are the key and spirit thread
To prove that life will all renew.

"Tell all of those who wish to know
The love and light of Source supreme,
The lesson from my trees will show
The Truth is clearer than your dream."

Loud Talk

From where I sit the train is filled
With bobbing heads of gray.
A younger man is on the phone,
And loudly, 'cross the way.

We learn about a business plan
We did not want to know.
He'll stay the night in NYC,
Leaving on the 'morrow.

The graying pates just shake their heads,
And some do turn and stare
To see the man who's rudely loud;
He can't be unaware.

But when some time has finally passed,
We're hearing not a sound.
His hand is tight upon his phone.
The train is underground.

WOOD AND HEART

A cabinet from the heart appeared
And gave its beauty to a room.
We marveled and we all revered
What hands and mind did thus exhume

From out a tree that passed in time,
But did not die and disappear.
It kept its inner grace confined
To be the cabinet that appeared.

True beauty can't be seen as one—
It takes another to be known.
The hands of skill left naught undone.
No longer is the tree alone.

MEDITATION

Before the light is done and gone
And raging ceases too,
There comes a time of prayerful thought
And seeing what is true.

And when I spend some time on this,
With meditative pause
I'll move within the noble light
Long past the primal cause.

When last I looked within my heart,
The only place of peace,
I found a portal to the Source
Where Love will never cease.

So now I tell you that my search
Is over and it's done.
I'll never need another quest
To see beyond the sun.

PASSING THOUGHTS

Late in life there are things I've learned–
That if you keep your loves too close,
There will be things in life not earned
By losing what you cherish most.

When old, the past is easily lost
And future thoughts come blooming late,
For when the spring has turned to frost,
We must succumb to spirit's fate.

And if the poet calls for rage
Against the dimming of the light,
We must remember life's a stage,
For what is next is past the fight.

There is much more to who we are
If only memory served us well
Where all of us could reach the star
That writes the story love will tell.

POET'S FIRE

The fire burns its bright this night
And sheds its light and heat.
But where is my poetic sight
To count my rhythm's beat?

Most hearths include the heart and home
And hold all thoughts within,
But fire burns a poet's tome,
So I must new begin.

I see the orange above the ash
And watch it settle down,
For in the color there's panache
That brightens rhyming's crown.

The sound must be a factor too
When snaps and crackles pop.
It takes my thought to where it's true
When meter seems to stop.

Beware, my friends, before a fire
When embers choose to die.
Let not your heart and mind retire
Before you say good-bye.

So this becomes an epitaph
For thoughts and embers too.
They ne'er will be a poet's path
If silent times are few.

Six Miles High

I see the earth from miles' high
Against the norm of common sense.
It happens every time I fly
And see the planet thus condense.

I ask the question from my perch,
Why is it we can't get along?
The answer perks from soulful search;
It's inward where all truths belong.

I oft look there in silent time
And know there is a mystic lock
That opens minds to what's sublime,
Though many see an opaque frock.

It's just a curtain, I declare,
And all are able if they choose
To push it free from everywhere.
A few will try, and most refuse.

Ojo Caliente

Earth's waters rise from deep within,
Releasing places that we've been,
Relaxing body, mind and soul
So once again the spirit's whole.

The mineral springs, both hot and cool,
Emerge and flow to gentle pools,
Creating balance 'tween all things
For water's sound lets nature sing.

The Posi Pueblo is nearby,
Though gone and crumbled to the eye,
Yet ancient spirits roam this land,
Anointing all with sacred sand.

I know there are the ancients here
With spirit forms that cause no fear.
I sense their wisdom in this place
That benefits the human race.

When I am gone from time and earth
I'll roam this land in spirit's birth.
If mortal life returns to me,
Return I will on bended knee.

CENTRAL PARK

Among the bricks and window stacks
Is nature at her best.
Who says within a city place
You'll not have Gaia's breast?

When pace and sound delay your thoughts,
A stroll resets your mind
To where a clear and placid calm
Belies the city's grind.

I stand in awe of what I see
So close to streets and lights,
For here I hear the crickets' call,
Yet see the building's heights.

'Tis here, my friend, you'll find a peace
That lingers past your walk.
Its grace will last within your heart
Though tucked in steel's frock.

To all who live in Gotham's clime,
Take time to be outside.
The parks and paths have ponds and grass
And nature to abide.

SHADOWS AND STARS

Behold the beauty sown in light
To bright the way to inner bliss
Upon the canvas of the night.
Before the darkness's good-night kiss.

The naked trees of wintertime
Pay homage in their silent prayer
To All That Is as Source sublime,
Their gowns of green no longer there.

We often ask to see the love
Of something greater than the mind.
A pristine sky and stars above
Are answers when the two combine.

LETTING GO

Letting go is often fearful
To the mind that sets a limit.
See not a box nor boundary
Lest you find yourself within it.

Be the freedom of your spirit
As it transcends the ego's greed.
Trust your heart and its connection
To Source within that won't mislead.

To follow true your creation
Reprise God's love from long ago.
A gift bequest from All That Is,
As truth above, a truth below.

Music of the Flowers

All sides in war all cry as ONE,
But little change does war imbue.
We make our hates where there are none
And pray for peace within a pew.

The hate within and war without
Will still the power of our grace
And leave us empty, filled with doubt,
Balanced on a shadow's face.

The genesis of hate is fear
In which we harbor mindless hurt.
We use our thoughts to harm and smear
And hide the truth within the dirt.

Hate lurks in minds and knows it's wrong
For all are ONE beyond a thought.
We must remember we're a song
Despite illusions we have wrought.

There is a way from out this spell
That we've created needlessly.
It's not a potion we can't quell;
It is a choice, a heart's decree.

To change your lives, just change your mind
And see what happens to your fear.
Your wound-up hate will then unwind
And spirit's peace will then appear.

All flowers then with fragrant scent
Will cast their pollen, drying tears.
So spirits then need not lament
The missing music of the spheres.

WAITING TIME

Tabled company, most unknown,
Furtive glances, exchanged or sown.
Aroma binds and flavor holds
The thoughts of strangers in the folds
Of mindless space and clinking glass.
Enough of that. She's here at last.

O CANADA

From Canada my dad did come
Across the border to the States.
He came for work when he was young
And also found his love's embrace.

His father came from Britain's heart,
A Midlands village in the west.
He lived a path he did not chart
For tragedy left life undressed.

He lost his family in a fire
And moved his roots to Canada.
'Twas there he found another pyre–
A fiery gal, my grandmama.

From them my dad was given life
And grew to manhood on the coast.
New Brunswick's living had its strife
But it became my father's host.

But rocks and roots must oft let go,
And Dad began his quest for more,
And to the States, with oats to sow,
He set his hopes on Boston's shore.

When I was small and just a shard,
To Canada we thus would go.
One uncle was a border guard,
Another farmed so long ago.

So now you know why I can say,
"O Canada, your rocks and root
Are part of me this very day,
And so to you a long salute."

Solitude

Upon the beach he stands alone,
But lonely he cannot abide.
There is a space between the two
Where mind decides the distance 'tween.

You cannot see where his stare starts
Or where it stops within his thought.
The distance is a grain of sand
Or all the oceans of his heart.

There is a clue beyond the sun
Behind his image on the sand.
Hold your focus a little more
And you will know that all are ONE.

The Art of Fall

Each breeze of fall creates her art
By choosing leaves to fly around.
Yellows float and crimsons dart,
The browns and oranges twist and bound.

Some colored piles are rococo
While others blend like palette's streak.
It changes when the breezes blow
With added colors in their peak.

To find a frame for autumn's grace
And hold its beauty for a time
You must imagine and embrace
That all of nature is a rhyme.

FRILLY LIMERICK

All women know men can be led
With lingerie in blushing red.
Some men however
Often endeavor
To peek before clothing is shed.

This surely is no passing fad
For always men have been glad
Of what women wear
And choose to share
That in public is often forbad.

I wonder where all this began.
Was it Folies Bergère, cancan?
Who added the lace?
A spice to the chase,
To catch us whenever we ran.

Some guys will try to fight back,
But smarts and cunning they lack.
They get an old book
From cranny and nook
Or play cards, perhaps some blackjack.

They go to their shop and their tools
Believing that they're not the fools.
They hammer a nail
Or fill up a pail
And trying to think up new rules.

Me thinks we should say where we stand
To prove that our head's not in sand.
If put on the spot,
Admit it or not,
Victoria's Secret is grand.

365 AND MORE

It's been a year since love was lost
From one who said "I do."
I oft would rage with tempests tossed
When thoughts of old came through.

'Tis true that time does conquer rage
And loss begins to wane,
And only then the Source's sage
Can soothe away the pain.

There were some signs, there're always signs,
From there to here direct.
Be quiet in the peaceful times;
It's then they do select.

She always sent her angels to
All those who needed love,
And I suspect today it's true
From angel bands above.

I do not wish her back to me
For she has other quests,
As I now do in mortal's sea
Before my tide's at rest.

They float upon the blue of heaven's floor
Above the desert's dry and distant street,
These steps of mystic mist that gods adore
When walking top the clouds in soft bare feet.
Dissolve they do, for spirits quickly pass
Attending to their realms and duties held.
Then Gaia in her nature smoothes the path
And gathers mists together in a meld.
From this she makes another downy cloud
Where spirits rest before the morning bright.
For soon they rush to gather and enshroud
The human pleas from prayers before God's light.
All this is from a painting of the sky,
And spirit's grace commands I say, "Oh my!"

THE RED CHAIR

I spent some time not long ago
Within the woods of primal time.
The wind was there, soft, to and fro,
As was the chill of northern clime.

But in the chair of red was peace.
I took some time to think and pray.
What came to me was a release
From straining thoughts that come each day.

The chair of red sustains a grace
For tuning in to something else
That's not at home but in this place,
And now it's mine. It's what I felt.

This is a chair that does divine
The solace that the spirit seeks.
By water's edge as I recline
I see life's truth where I can peek.

ANGEL IN THE WINDOW

They were tiny panes, I admit,
And though my mind says it's not so,
I'm sure I saw an Angel sit
There in the window, all aglow.

It couldn't be! I know it's said
That Angels rarely can be seen,
But what I saw had wings outspread,
Or so it seemed with glass between.

Maybe it's a light reflection,
A sparkle of the sun's bright light,
Maybe too, an imperfection
Set in the glass, however slight.

Just as I went to turn away,
I heard her voice within my mind.
It softly wished, as if to pray,
"A lasting peace to all mankind."

The words were calming, halcyon,
But what was I supposed to do?
"Say it," she said, "to everyone,
Those here and there, to all unto."

"Am I," said I, "to represent
A spirit's wish to all I see?
I'm only one, and though well-meant,
Some hearts are filled with apathy."

"Besides," I said, "how do you say
To everyone and everywhere,
An Angel asked me to convey
A lasting peace alike a prayer?"

The Angel said, "Be not concerned,
For those will hear who have the ear.
They'll listen to and then discern
The peace of truth that will appear."

"Whose truth is that?" I did implore
And looked around the window frame
To try to see the Angel more,
When then her answer did proclaim:

"It is a truth from Source above,
So heed the thoughts' phenomenon.
Know joy and truth equate as love,
A triad essence of the One."

I felt this truth, right from the start.
It energized and set ablaze
The light that rested in my heart,
And then she said this loving phrase:

"A single word with love intent
Said unto those you do not know
Creates a light that's ambient
When you, as stranger, say hello."

I held my breath to hear some more.
These words of truth were most profound,
But it was silent as before . . .
Before the Angel came around.

I'm sure there was an Angel there,
Out the window and to the right
But as I looked beyond the glare,
The shining light had taken flight.

So thus I share with you and your,
The truth an Angel left behind,
A special wish that will endure:
"A lasting peace to all mankind."

In the Air

The ache of spring is in the air
Despite the chill of winter's fare.
I see it in the buds of trees
Whose pokes from 'neath the twigs do please.

For me a sadness in each spring
When birth and growth cannot re-bring
The energy of parted souls
Whose lives we shared with gentle strolls.

But then I know, I truly know
Life's light forever keeps its glow,
For when complete, form goes away
And spirit laughs and plays the play.

We who stay must understand
That, short or long, life's ever grand
And ceases not despite the shift
Of back and forth in cosmic drift.

But back to spring and its rebirth
With life profound from sentient earth—
Both warmth and light do bright the stage,
Releasing all from winter's cage.

DOOM AND GLOOM

Let's choose some words and play a game
To fit our national mood.
For some it's doom and some it's blame
Where most are misconstrued.

But I am sad in what I read
For gloom is part of it.
Investors think the growing seed
Is tarred within a pit.

That may be true and times are tough
And loss does come to mind,
But don't you think we have enough
To not get more entwined?

We really have a lot to count
For those who keep the score,
And when it's bad, we all surmount
The issues we abhor.

When global markets scrape the tanks
And numbers breach and fall,
Let's change our thoughts to giving thanks
For what we have at all.

We have so much, we're spoiled kids,
Complaining all the time.
Comparing us to real "skids,"
Our lot is most sublime.

Can we not go from east to west
And turn and then head back
Without a stop to even rest,
No border stops to track?

Do we not have a power source
Without a thought each day?
To me that is a gift perforce
And something we should weigh.

Do we not have a freedom's grace
To say what all we please?
And let our thoughts then interface
With others in degrees.

We have a vote where some do not,
And choice to make it so.
Too many say, "Oh, I forgot
To pull the lever row."

I'll bet with thought a list would come
And blend within your mind—
So many gifts where we succumb
And be as if we're blind.

There are so many things we need
To say we're thankful for.
The sun is one, and flower's seed,
And mountains and the shore.

A gentle rain is in there too
As is an Eagle's screech.
Let's not forget the morning dew
And those who like to teach.

So when we say we've not enough,
Complaining here and there,
Perhaps we need to call our bluff
And make the choice to share.

A thank-you is oft hard to do,
And some think it means weak,
But we should say it and pursue
This way to always speak.

So I will end this post this day
With lofty thoughts in mind
And hope that all who read will say
'Tis gloom I leave behind.

Young Love

When young love's love does not succeed
And other choices must prevail,
The loss for each may oft impede
Fulfillment of their dreaming tale.

But from an age of many years
Emotion wans and knowing knows
That love's not lost despite the fears,
And knows, in fact, the loving grows.

In memories of a youthful love
I say to all: enjoy the now,
For when and if push comes to shove,
The choices made are right somehow.

When youth and love are blended to
Each other's beat of loving heart,
Do not forsake what's always true
Despite the fact you are apart.

Remember in the once of time
Young love endures with thoughts sublime.
As hearts would ache when ending came,
Old memories pass with what's to blame.

WAVES OF LEAVES

I watched the roiling waves of green
Devoid of shore and sandy scene.
They rolled and tumbled with the wind,
In ebb and flow advance, rescind.

The graceful waves are from the breeze
That moves the leaves among the trees,
Just like the ocean's waves on shore.
My gaze is wanting, hoping more.

But here there is no tidal force;
It's just the wind in blowing course.
It moves in gusts of rhythmic dance
And holds my gaze long past a glance.

THE WHISTLE

I heard a distant whistle blow,
'Twas mournful in its wail,
But that was in a dream, I think,
Where truths will oft prevail.

The whistle's call was real enough,
At least within my mind.
Its empty sound reminded me
Of loss in distant time.

It's time, they say, that cures all ills
And time that tames the heart,
But time can't take the pain away
When scars do tear apart.

The pain of then, so long ago,
When towers burned and fell
Renews its hurt when names are read
And clappers ring the bell.

The month's the same, the year is not,
When I too lost a son.
But grief is grief when all seems lost;
It is for everyone.

But now I choose, as all must do,
To honor life above
And let him go to heaven's things
And send to him my love.

I heard a distant whistle blow,
'Twas lonely in its wail,
But that was in my dream, I think,
Where truths do oft prevail.

ORLANDO

Not known is the moment.
We never know the time
When beckoned calls are sent
To old and those in prime.

All we can do is pray
For those who passed above.
We know for all someday
That home is one of love.

To understand the hate
And seeing all the dead,
My mind cannot relate
When reason is misled.

Why must we go through this
So many times this life?
The dead embrace a bliss.
The living live with strife.

My questions ache with pain.
No answers do I know.
The killer was insane,
And ISIS his credo.

No answers come with thought.
No reason I can know.
We live with what is wrought.
Rest in peace, Orlando.

BALANCE

Consider this, inquiring friend,
There's no beginning and no end.
There's only balance, out of time,
A mystic concept much sublime.

Exempt your mind from granite plight
That stays your thinking from the light,
Then loose all structure from your mind
To keep your mystery undefined.

It is within our intellect
To understand and then reflect
That something holds us in a grace
To freely move from place to place.

It is a poise we cannot see
That compensates, in this theory,
For any movement anywhere
To keep the status wheresoe'er.

Not even thought can interfere,
Disturbing place or atmosphere,
For there is something balancing
The butterfly who flaps its wing.

The winter snow and infant's dream
Are also part of life's routine;
All need balance, to equalize
For drift and growth or blink of eyes.

Let us assume this Universe
Is perfect balance and diverse
And in this form of symmetry
There comes a knowing certainty.

All atoms, quarks, and humankind
Have orbits and are intertwined
To all the others' frequency,
A masterpiece in artistry.

Again assume a paradigm,
Omniscient, a mover prime,
That set in motion everything
And gave the tone of Aum to ring.

Now take the step of further thought,
What keeps this balance from onslaught
Of random pandemonium
Disturbing equilibrium?

There only is one answer to
This complicated spirit glue,
A cosmic field unified
By something simple, undenied.

It's love.

GAIA'S LAMENT

When eyes of youth look up at us
And ask what do we see,
The answer lies within our love
Of nature's land and sea.

All children know that deep within
Their spirit is attuned
To trees and plants and furry things
And flowers that festoon.

Kids need adults to take the step
And point to what's outdoors,
To see what crawls and buzzes 'round
Or washes up on shore.

There'll come a time in children's lives
When growing they forget
To see the stars and sniff the breeze
Or feel a bare foot wet.

But there is hope within our hearts
When actions are profound.
So keep the vision in your mind
When children are around.

Then take them out to feel the earth
And its connecting force
For then they'll know the grace of all–
That nature is the source.

THE MASTERS TAUGHT

What is our spirit telling us
When we true listen to its words?
Is it a truth where we adjust
Or something that we think absurd?

Both what I know and what I think
Are different from my thoughtful mind
Where thinking oft connotes a wink,
But knowing is a thought refined.

The Masters always speak of Now
And let the past and future go.
Be elegant and disavow
The thoughts that held us long ago.

Illusion is the ego's force,
A construct of our human mind.
It is a path and compass course
For sleepy souls of humankind.

The Masters tell us to awake
And thus embrace the inner heart
And live the NOW to not forsake
What spirit's heart will true impart.

SHOUT TO THE WIND

Shout to the wind and say your truth
And hear it back to check it out.
Then gnaw it clean with mind and tooth;
Make sure it's pure and with no doubt.

The wind will take your truth and sigh
And send it past those hearing not.
They'll know not why it passes by
With reason lost that they forgot.

So shout into the wind, my friend,
And worry not what will be heard.
The time will come when time will end
And truth will be the primal word.

Snow Shoe

The silence in a forest white
Belies the space of mind's delight
When walking in another's track
Upon a snow that's shrinking back.

There is no sound except the joy
Within my heart that does deploy
Into a smile of prayer and grace,
Proclaiming this a sacred place.

I walked with friends on snow new found,
A crystal mist that stays to ground
And warms my soul within its cold
As I traverse its beauty's fold.

ONCE AGAIN

And once again a hatred came to kill.
Once again the innocent lay and die.
Once again ISIS, the scourge of Islam,
Embraced the bomb to make Earth's children cry.

Noble Belgium, we share your painful loss.
Your pain and fear reminds us of our past
When planes destroyed our trading towers high.
'Twas then we hoped the twins would be the last.

Oh, ISIS, you are not Mohammad's kin!
The Prophet weeps and aches within his grave
For what you do in Islam's name and shame.
Know all the world calls you Satan's slave.

Once again, great Lord, never once again.
Let the carnage, the pain and sorrow end.
We are all spirits of the same love's gift.
Please show the way for conflicts to transcend.

Let all the candles of the world ignite
And let the flames of love embrace the hate
To end the cause of pain with Source's light
So human kind can be its sacred fate.

Jefferson's Lament

One two three seven, all Trump needs
To heed his ego's call.
But there are forces with new seeds
To cause this bigot's fall.

Some say he started this pursuit
To guild his family's name.
It is a claim he does refute
Despite increasing fame.

So where does that leave politics?

(pause and think)

This poem can now not end.
It knows the way some lunatics
Can set the future's trend.

Now if you say that I'm not fair
And Donald is the way,
Just read his words and then compare
What Jefferson would say.

Before the sun lets go its light

There comes a time of thought.

So hold your glance within the bright

And let your joy be caught.

LEE'S LEDGE

A canyon, once below a time,
Did forge a course of grace sublime,
A vision from the mind of God
And sculpted out of time and sod.

Its layered depth of sand and stone
Would be its grandeur's undertone,
As eons' count and water's slice
Now manifest this paradise.

An earthly place of peace and rest
For all who journey on the quest
To be the sight of humankind
And see the centuries intertwined.

The canyon's walls and rocky schist
Are music and the lyricist
To write the songs of epoch lines
Etched in the sides of rock designs.

To understand the nature here
One must move inward and be clear
That Gaia too expresses love
Through vistas grand below, above.

The melodies within these walls
Resound with light and shadow falls.
They sing to those whose privileged place
Finds them attuned to sacred space.

It is exemption to be here
Away from social, civil fear
And all the hurts left in your mind
Along with things you've left behind.

The canyon's call is powerful,
A mystic magnet, beautiful.
A sandstone ledge or lucid dream
Connects the soul to God Supreme.

CHOICES

Beyond the love of living life
With all its joys and seeming strife,
There comes a time when we must choose
A way to live so love accrues.

It takes some thought to understand
The life within is what is grand.
The other way is where we find
That not all the choices will be kind.

But there are lessons to be learned
In all our choices, I've discerned.
We may not like the tasks we chose,
But it's the way the spirit grows.

So when you think and when you pray,
Give thanks for gifts you have this day,
For that will let you be the light
Which will confirm your choice is right.

Now if we choose to thus refuse,
That love is not the choice we use;
There's never judgment from the Source,
Though someday we may choose remorse.

Be not afraid in time and space.
No life is always grace and lace.
No ego ever had control.
Love is the power of the soul.

Primal Thought

Beware the black of fear and graying light
When earthly reason cannot see the bright.
For now's the time to bide your mind and soul
As spirit swallows all illusions whole.

Now move your thoughts to where it's empty space
To thus acknowledge true the wholesome grace
Of joy and wisdom coming from the Source,
And sadness and old pain have no recourse.

Love holds us in the brace of lasting peace.
It is a blessed gift that does release
The primal thought of life you've chosen now
As right and just and what you did avow.

Avow you did, before the council's light,
Before your body formed into its might,
For density is hard to comprehend
When spirit and a form in matter blend.

The poets of all time will tell us truth
When preaching to the learned and the youth.
For death does not diminish what they say;
It is the listening mind that does decay.

Dinosaur Limerick

There once lived a big dinosaur
Whose life was all legend and lore.
He lived in the snow.
Scientists say no,
But there they found bones to restore.

It happened way south at the pole.
Researchers discovered a hole.
There in an ice bed
From tail to head
Were fossilized bones in a row.

They're two hundred million years old,
These bones that our science beholds.
With tiny front feet
And powerful teeth
This creature ate meat, we are told.

Now science is placed on the spot.
No Ripley's *Believe It or Not*,
Not even a wink,
Can change what we think.
The Antarctic was once quite hot.

BLUEBONNETS BOLD

Bold blossoms blue stand proud above their green.
They grow in strength and know their light is seen
By all who motor by or stop to gaze
Into this garden of wonder, a maze.

Color binds attention, and form holds grace,
Attracting heart and spirit to this place.
The flowers stand as one and separate too
As symbols of the noble ones, too few,

Who come to see and hold this place in love,
Responding to an essence from above.
Sweet nectar is the wine of blossoms blue,
Sipping through the lips of zephyrs new.

Tell all who pass here, fast or walking by:
The fragrance of the flowers glorify
The spirit of the earth and nurtured seed
That blossoms into beauty when we need.

A Cup of Tea

I had a cup of tea today
And thought about some times before.
The brew beheld a memory frayed,
Yet opened up an inner door.

This happens now from time to time
From sounds or songs and errant thoughts.
When feelings seep from deep in mind,
Old choices rise and what we've wrought.

Age always tempers visions past
And comforts thoughts from long ago
Where most were hopes that didn't last
But cast a light in love's shadow.

The Age of Light

I am the now among the light
But daily play in planet's night
Where souls oft gasp a wonder's breath
When learning light is never death.

But we do dwell in moment's time
For matter is a finite clime.
Yet when we shed our form and thought,
The mind can never be distraught.

There is a balance 'tween the two
In order for the spirit true
To keep the Logos and the soul
From being separate from the whole.

How does that fit with dogma's trick
Which many souls now see as slick?
It doesn't fit, so do not try;
A freeing mind lets spirit fly.

Not all the words of old are wrong,
But light creates a different song.
Old tunes have truth as new ones do,
But only one brings what is new.

Aquarian we call this age
Where knowing beings set the stage
For all of us to be the play
In lighted garments all array.

THOUGHT

'Twas the day before New Year's
And all over the world
The people were hoping
That love would unfurl.

As I sat in my chair
And wondered out loud,
Could this be the time
When peace is avowed?

I looked at the headlines
And watched some TV.
It didn't seem likely,
I'm sure you'll agree.

When out from the spirit
There came a great thought:
If we change what we think,
Can we change what we wrought?

The answer that came was
The truth, I am sure,
For beginnings and ends
Are often obscure.

So beware what you think
In life at this time.
Creation is simple
When thought is sublime.

Global Warming

Of course there is no climate change,
The ignorant will say.
High heat and cold are never strange;
It's all in nature's play.

Some others say it's not our fault
The arctic ice will melt.
Mankind cannot be nature's halt
Despite some changes felt.

For me, it seems that ignorance
Is pandering to greed.
The rich may beg the difference,
But change is now the seed.

And when it warms to melt the ice
And seas begin to rise,
The ignorant will then say twice,
"Well, that's a big surprise."

When some exclaim with deep concern,
This change is tragic news,
Then I will say we didn't learn
We are what we abuse.

THE EUCHARIST

The Eucharist of light descends to all
Who choose to see its rays from deep within.
Beyond the leaves of doubt and pending fall
There shines a knowing thought that must begin.
So many times in life we tread the path
Below the canopy of spirit's light.
How many times have we ignored the lash
Of truth to stay as dogma's parasite?
Live in the now beneath the orb of grace
And let all judgments go to where they end
And know that all we see is in its place
Despite the fact we may not comprehend.
Rejoice, my friends, the world's bathed in love;
We see it clearly, through the trees above.

OLD MEN, YOUNG MEN

What old men share with youthful friends
Beyond the toast of decent wines
Are truths of life and river bends
When floating o'er a river's tines.

So blessed was I, the older one,
To be with youth and their play
As we traversed what nature spun
And plied the currents this fine day.

One said to me not long ago
When boating on a flowing stream,
"Nothing's better than this, you know."
His love of nature was his dream.

Another time, this one on snow,
Youth in front and blazing trail.
Next by age, then me so slow.
Of course, I was the elder snail.

But I did write a poem that time
From all the joy I carried back.
It was a couplet and in rhyme
In thanks to youth for making tracks.

But that was then and this is now
And sadness weeps within the mind.
We'll all go on, that's life somehow,
Though dying young seems so unkind.

There's only one, a younger soul,
That I have loved and I have lost
While on this mortal earthly stroll,
That I mourn more that he has crossed.

It was my son, when young, who died,
And now I ask him for a grace
To welcome youth to Heaven's side
And guide them through that other place.

RHETORIC

I heard his words from somewhere dark.
He said to me that I should fear
That things are bad, the future stark.
He can fix it; we'll persevere.

From where I stand and where I sit
I see us strong and proud and fit.
I do not see our vision grim
And many other pseudonyms.

Fearful is what we must not be.
It gives away our reasoned mind.
Let go of fear, then truth is free
And you will have a life refined.

No one man or no one woman
Can make it great for every soul.
It's up to us, it's our élan
To make the choices and keep control.

Nature's Walk

My walk began at forest's edge, beneath a blue dream sky.
The morning air was crisp, no dust came from the dry.
I looked around at nature, knowing I would find
Her rhythm in a rock, and songs within her rhyme.

I heard it first upon the path, walking slowly, not too far.
It faded in and out of mind like a distant twinkling star.
Then louder came its gentle tone, uniquely humming mild.
When tuning in to nature's sound your spirit is beguiled.

I hear the bubbling sparkle of a trickling tiara stream
That slides o'er stone and granite bead crowning Gaia queen.
You feel it in the ebbing wind with all its names that please,
"Refreshing," "cooling," "gentle," special kinds of breeze.

You see it in the flora and the rainbows of the flower,
As blossoms bloom with color in a natural sculptured bower.
You taste sweet nature's breath when fragrance fills the air,
With tiny pollens of her heart, perfumes of scented prayer.

Nature's essence is profound; her truth comes when you listen
To the dew that's on the grass, and to the sunlight glisten,
With squinting crystals in the bright that hide when it is warm
But then return the liquid life in shower and in storm.

There's tiny life upon the ground, in trails of hurried ants.
It's also on and in the healing medicine plants.
I find it often in the trees, amid a darting of delight
As playful fluttering feathered ones put magic in their flight.

There are troubled things to know from the scars of human reach.
We need to heed the warning shrill of the Owl's casting screech.
Nature's sound speaks many tongues to tell us there is trouble,
For in the print of humankind the future reeks in rubble.

But on my walk I shall not dwell upon predicted bad
For it would change my wooded walk and change my joy to sad.
In all my walks, on many paths, even ones without a tree,
I choose to find the joy of life, for nature lives in me.

Skiing

Within my glide on carpets white
There is the frame of lasting bright
Where worries end and laughs begin
With nature's breeze as violin.
Her music guides me in this joy
On ridges groomed in corduroy.
So down the slope I slide and swoon
On melodies of nature's tune.

The Question

Past the days of illusion's dream
Come rhymes and thoughts of spirit's truth:
That nothing here we see is real
Despite the eyes that say it's proof.

So where do mind and body go
To find the essence of our Source,
Where truth is told and nothing more,
So we can hold an earthly course?

We've all been here in form before
As other lives with other names.
Each time we've said we'll grow to love
A promise made to play the games.

My question's not, When do we take
The final breath and go on home?
It is, Do we, have that as choice
To end our free-will mortal roam?

Gordian's knot is held within
Of tightened thought and consequence,
But when untied with personal choice,
No judgment's made in preference.

ICE STORM

The ice has come to coat the trees
In prism's slice of colored light.
I must await the shaking breeze
To free the bark and buds forthright.

Refraction has its counterpart
Within the sound of crackling ice.
It lets your mind and thought depart
To feel the sound as it clinks thrice.

For some there is no joy in cold,
No beauty seen on slippery street.
For others this is coated gold
With greetings to the freezing sleet.

But I am one that sees it all
From when it's warm and when it's not,
In spring, the summer and the fall.
I also see in the winter's blot.

'Tis nature and her craft of art
That decorates a winter's scene.
Despite our hopes of mind and heart
Ice is the glaze of grace's sheen.

Four Old Friends

When four old friends meet once again,
Remembering a youthful past,
It is a time of laughs and fun
With hopes of more and lives steadfast.

Some fifty years have traveled by;
Careers at end and hair now gray.
The four old friends did walk along
Sharing thoughts of another day.

It is a truth that life is change
And all must seek their special road.
It's also true that once a friend
It lasts for life, a gift bestowed.

BILL OF RIGHTS

I looked upon a bill today
And I was taken by surprise.
It had no stamp to mark it paid.
It never will and that is wise.

The list was those of noble thought.
Ten in a line and in a row
And numbered in the Roman way
From I to X in even flow.

The first one was about some things
We rarely give a thought about:
The right of faith and gathered groups
And saying things by speaking out.

Protection next was on the list
And bearing arms, if so you choose.
It talked about militias too,
So no one's freedom is abused.

The third one had to do with force,
Of soldiers living in your space.
It could not be without consent
Unless a law does grant the grace.

The fourth one had to do with search
Of you, your home and papers too
Unless there was a reasoned cause
That power may not misconstrue.

The fifth one was a longer one
Dealing with one's self-conviction.
We have the right to talk or not
When accused of malediction.

The next one dealt with one's arrest
And a quick and speedy trial.
The right to counsel was there too
To tell the court of one's denial.

The seventh was a master one.
In all the suits of common law
Your peers decide your truth or not.
No court can change what juries saw.

The eighth is one of great import
To keep us from excessive fines
Or punished in a cruel, strange way
If we're convicted of a crime.

The ninth is all about the rights
Set in the Constitution's list,
But even rights not listed there
Are equal and both co-exist.

Ten talks about the document,
And if the wording is not there,
The states and people keep the rights
So that there is a balance fair.

No money pays this sacred bill;.
The rights are free and can't be bought.
They're guarantees for one and all,
Paid by the blood from those who fought.

Manger Child

O manger child of Christmas morn,
Archangels bowed when you were born.
The holy light from cherubim
Graced your spirit in Bethlehem.

O manger child, please grace our heart
That sees your stable birth impart
A sacred truth for all to share:
Love is the answer and the prayer.

Amen, my child. Amen, my Lord.
Hear harmony in Christmas chord
From bells and voices of the young
With songs of heart in carols sung.

Oh, sing, my child, your song of light
That we may see all mornings bright,
Especially this season of
The Christmas spirit as above.

We sing, we sing what joy does bring
From breaking dawn to evening,
We sing along with choral throng
And chapel chimes 'til evensong.

O mystic child, upon this day
Your love is heard in pull of sleigh,
In ringing bells, and white snowdrift
And presents wrapped as Christmas gift.

Your gift to us, to all of us
From child's heart harmonious:
A simple truth we can redeem.
Love is the gift, the gift supreme.

HOMEWARD SPRING

"'The time has come,' the Walrus said,
'To talk of many things'"–
Of heading home where oven's bread
Is like the eastern spring.

For me, my roam and time away
And journey cross the plain
Was more for warmth, but I can't stay
Where heat's a daily gain.

So now I head to eastern shore
To see the tulip's spring,
Remembering the sound and more
Of peepers' birthing ring.

Spring comes with joy to those of us
Who honor species far.
Each prides their place with knowing trust
Despite a winter's scar.

This is a time to be aware
Of powered place and phrase.
Each spring's a grace and lasting prayer,
A loving light ablaze.

GOALS AND AGE

There comes a time in all our dreams
When we let go and sigh,
"It could have been!" We had the means
To try and try and try.

There must be something in our hopes
That lets us seek the goal.
We learned techniques and know the ropes
But then we lose control.

Perhaps it's age or other stuff
That loosens a sure grip,
And we let go with no rebuff
The goal we think we skip.

But I have learned throughout the years,
When letting go, I find
The goal I lost then reappears
As new and redefined.

So what's the lesson in this thought
That I must now embrace?
It is to never be distraught
When things seem out of place.

LAUREL RIDGE

Upon Ohayo's high rock ledge
A vision once was held
To build a home, on just the edge,
Where family hearts could dwell.

'Tis high enough to feel the breeze
Of zephyrs traveling by;
They play and dance and get the trees
To poke the blue dream sky.

As time went on, the structure grew
Into a hearth and home
With wood and stone, from drawings true,
And land to freely roam.

When craftsmen left their art to view
And season through the years,
The grace of place became the glue
To hold what now appears.

The choice was then to choose a name
To last forever more,
A noble name that does proclaim
A vista to adore.

Then out from thought and lofty lair
A name became a bridge
Connecting hearts to true declare:
Its name is Laurel Ridge.

MATHARE SLUMS

I walked along the shacks of tin
And felt my mind in disbelief.
A sadness came from deep within
With throbbing thoughts of no relief.

One cannot know the lives of some
Without the heart to open wide
And see that all of us are ONE
Beyond the culture and the pride.

A million souls in one foul place,
Where sewers slide along the feet,
A liquid stench of winding lace
On what the children call the street.

Some little ones peek from the door
To watch the strangers walking by.
How can I pass and thus ignore
That living here is cry and die?

The children look and wave to each
And say to those who smile back,
"How are you, Sir?"—their words that reach
The heart and soul that knows the lack.

Each slippery step from me in mire
Presented scenes from life's latrine:
Cooking o'er a charcoal fire
And keeping self and children clean.

My spirit ached when last I stepped
Away from lives I'll never see,
When out of sight I silent wept
And thanked the All it isn't me.

ALONG THE ROAD

Bachelor buttons and Queen Anne's lace
Astride the ways to every place.
Crocheted in white, the doily blooms
Beside the lanky Bachelor plumes.
Both thrive where few would like to be
Along the road for all to see.
A gift of grace for passersby,
Their whites and blues reflect the sky.

FRIENDSHIP

I spent some time with friends just now.
It took me back before my birth.
I do not know the why or how,
But I did feel their spirit's mirth.

I knew them then with other names
And we were clustered in a group.
One day in joyful talk and games
We talked about a mortal loop.

In spirit talk, that means again
To come on back to earthly space
And play with time and choice refrain
And plan each life with guidance grace.

So we did choose our separate ways
And dove into the womb of time,
Accepting growth and dense delays
Depending on our karma's rhyme.

But let me bring us back to now
And all the joys of friendship's love.
By laughs and hugs we did avow
What is below is love above.

Autumn Times

Who knows which leaf will leave its stem
When autumn breezes blow.
Do angels know, or higher yet,
When looking down below?

Fall winds are cool and gentle too
To brush the leaves off trees.
One here, two there, and then a group—
A sprinkling; floating spree.

Are leaves, like man, who pass when done
Expecting something more?
And is this knowing 'neath the bark
When they must seek the floor?

Within the glory of their green
There lies a splendor bright.
There's crimson reds and mottled gold.
It is a magic sight.

It's Begun

It has begun, the grasp of snow
To mark the winter's clime.
It comes in white to set the glow
For creatures at this time.

The trees no more in silhouette
Against a sky of blue,
They're bright in white as statuette
Before the snow's adieu.

Rejoice, my friends, the cold is here
For just a moment's time,
For next is when the spring appears.
The cycle is sublime.

Visits, a Sonnet

What is this? This nothing I hear and feel.
It was not here just a moment ago.
Just then it seemed that only noise was real
With chattered talk and din—a loud tableau.
There was the clink on glass and plates to clean
And conversation's noise around the room.
All families come with sound when they convene
To tell of life and laughter they exhume.
We oft forget to hold the silent space
That disappears within the clattered noise.
When gone, it leaves no sign, no note, no trace
But reappears when sound has lost its poise.
With children present silence leaves to roam
But then returns when grandkids head on home.

WANDERING FEARS

There are the sounds that darkness brings
That hold the mind to what it thought,
But we must let the crying sing
So sadness will not be what's wrought.

Forget the dark; it cannot be
For light is power in our sight.
Just try it once and you will see
Awareness then will set you free.

But back to sounds that have no form.
No shape, as yet, that we can know,
But when you love, there is no storm
Despite the tempest and the show.

I heard a sound within the dark;
It came with peace and arms outstretched.
It could have been a kind remark,
But that would make my fear far fetched.

Winter's Last

Winter's back this April month
Though warm was here a day ago.
I should have known that this would be
For spring arrives so very slow.

I see the Crocus poking through
The thawing earth of early spring.
But then a cold from farther north
Proclaims that winter still has sting.

But I still have a shed of wood
And logs to burn within their place.
A fire then will heat my room
And end the cold without a trace.

TREE PEOPLE

I found some people in a tree
But then I knew that they were me.
They are my son's twin daughters planned
And I the one with children grand.

I think that trees like kids to climb
And poets then to find the rhyme
To tell the story of ascent
Into the tree when knees are bent.

With them upon the limbs of bark
Lets me below make this remark,
"Be careful, kids, you're high enough,
The higher limbs are thin and rough,

For elder me and you so young
To get you out of high branch rung."
My worry was forever naught
And my concern thus overwrought.

The kids so nimble as they are
Did swing to ground that was not far.
And I as "Pop" did look away
As the kids went off to play.

I'm thinking of a saw I know
To cut the limb that's way below.
And if they ask, "Why did you cut?"
"Your Grannie's threat to kick my butt."

THE HEART WITHIN

My mind is sad by what I read
Within the papers and online.
There're hurts and fights and altered seed
Where systems fail and all's entwined.

There're shouts and threats and curses too
Along with tears and others' pain.
There're legal things, some false, some true,
That make some wrongs and laws remain.

But deep within I know it's right.
I know this is the way things are
Until we each embrace the light
And see that love's the avatar.

To always see when eyes are blind
First look within your searching heart,
But not from where it's tied to mind
But where it's open and apart.

Once there you'll find your scroll of soul
And too your light that shines within.
It's there your spirit light is whole
And you'll come back time and again.

Tell Me the Truth

"Tell me the truth.
Are we not ONE?
Why is your heart closed when mine is open?
Why am I hungry when you are full?
Why do I see dying young as normal
And you see it as a surprise?
Can you help me to laugh like you do?
What is it like to have enough?
I am you and you are me.
Is this not true?
Tell me the truth!"

Spring Hopes Eternal

A gentle rain has come and gone
And early birds now chirp and sing.
Their chatter is the season's song
That welcomes in a birthing spring.

Some buds are near but not yet seen
As warmth, like aches, both comes and goes.
Soon early bursts will have their green;
Then colors come as flowers grow.

The Daffodils don't seem to mind
When poking through the earthen cold.
The Crocus are a kindred kind,
A hardy species, always bold.

If April is the cruelest time,
So too is March and December.
Some other months, not so sublime
From winter winds, I remember.

So when you look upon the land
That sees that spring has not come yet,
It will be soon and will be grand;
Earth's angels know the time is set.

THE CONCLAVE

A sea of black in pates of red
Convenes to talk in ancient tongue,
To seek the one upon whose head
The ruling mitre crown is hung.

'Tis fate and faith and bargain's tools
That choose the one who now must head
The cardinal corps and vaults of rules.
He's gowned in white until he's dead.

Would that the Spirit find the one
So blackened smoke would turn to white.
There's only one as champion
To lead the flock for future's sight.

When crimsoned shoes are finally filled
And blind obedience secure,
The one in white will try to build
New ways to keep the faithful pure.

Blessings on you, new pope to come.
You have traditions old and new,
So choose a path that's premium
Despite objections from the few.

And thus upon the rock you stand
In fragrant truth and visions cast.
You are the one, now in command.
Reform the now, repair the past.

Sir Winston

It is with thought I sit and write
To pair with words a work of art
And see its grace with light's insight
By auguring a noble chart.

The captured look 'neath homburg hat
And Cuban leaf pursed 'tween the lips
Belie his wit on this and that
Plus deeds of war and battleships.

Our history tells us what he's done
And holds his place of honor due.
He is Great Britain's favored son,
A fabled knight whose heart was true.

We know his life from history,
But what's his thought here drawn with skill?
The answer stays a mystery
Within the art of ink and quill.

Sir Winston's life began, we know,
In Blenheim Castle's noble rife.
'Twas Woodstock there in grand chateau,
And Woodstock here in artist's life.

SKIES OF GOLD

Bright skies of gold announce the law
Of beauty's passage past the fall.
The trees of life with branches cleared,
Once gold themselves when fall premiered.
But now they pause for season's snow
Awaiting buds to green and grow.
The souls of man have too their gold
In skies of time as all grow old.

RIVER RIDE

To float, to glide, astride, and slide
Upon the river's surface side
With friends and talk and laughter too—
These times are true, but all too few.

The river calls from fathom's place
O'er depths and flow we must retrace,
Returning to the put-in point
Where nature's crown will thus anoint
The souls who push 'gainst current's flow
And fight the wind in heading blow.

When last we dock and kayak's out,
I know the joy without a doubt
To float, to glide, astride, and slide
Where friends and nature coincide.

RED-HEADED WOODPECKER

I heard a thump and knew the worst.
A bird had struck my windowpane.
The morning sun's reflection's curse
Did hide a flight that was in vain.

With tuft of red upon her head
And black and white and yellowed plumes
She lay so still. Her life now dead.
Her nature gone. Her flight entombed.

I picked her up so light in weight
And gave a loving soft caress.
A fatal flight, a saddened fate.
I hoped she passed without duress.

I wondered if the ALL did know,
And was a spirit bird alive?
Were all her colors now aglow,
And were there angels at her side?

Robin's Song

I finally heard the Robin sing
And yet the clime seems not like spring.
It's been a winter, harsh and hard,
And snow still covers half the yard.

Do you suppose it's climate change
Denied by those with minds deranged?
The souls of science keep a track
And Congress says it has our back.

So worry not 'bout dying bees
And ice-shelf melt and rising seas,
A snowy east and dry out west.
It is not true we've fouled our nest.

So as I hear the Robin sing
I hope her song will bring on spring.
We then can put our heads in sand
And rest assured our future's grand.

Truth in Aging

Since poetry is part of life
And I find joy in rhyme,
I'll speak my thoughts this special night
On how I've changed with time.

There're many things I know as true
These senior years, et al.
The first one is the memory goes,
The rest I can't recall.

There are four ages of each life
Where we do oft excel.
They're teens and youth and middle age,
The last, "You're looking well."

You know you're getting older
When knots you can't untie
And more things ache or nothing fits
And people call you spry.

I have my meds like Lipitor
Or something just the same
To watch my H and L.D.L.
So clogs will not remain.

It's funny how things change around
From youth and being slim.
What fat I have is in my waist,
My hair is what is thin.

When young, we ran when walk would do
To speed us on the road
Of life and love forever more
Before careers plateaued.

We've all become our destiny
With more, for sure, to come.
I've disappointments and some pride
Of actions I've begun.

But when I stop to think with thought
The things I think were done,
There're many things I know were right
And some were yarns I've spun.

There comes a time in all our years
When we look back at youth.
Some memories fade and others hold
Not always with the truth.

I'm grayer now and wrinkled too
And many friends are gone
To Heaven's field of blissful truth
Where every day's a song.

We'll all get there somehow, someday
And memory will come back.
No glasses then to see who's there
To know it's Bill or Jack.

Growing old is never easy,
Neither is a passing,
But there is joy in all our lives
Living, loving, laughing.

I need new ears with batteries,
And walk with sticks and canes.
My ups and downs come with a grunt,
My legs have varicose veins.

Some teeth are gone and some have caps
And I oft limp and ache,
But how I love my past-noon naps
And when I take my breaks.

Some youngsters call me elderly
And others call me "Sir."
The years do give me clarity
Though sight is oft a blur.

I do not know what's held in store
Beyond this passing night.
I do for certain know a truth:
Old age is filled with light.

But let me keep us in the now
Where life should always be.
So, I look good and you the same,
I'm sure you will agree.

But just in case that is not true
I'll fib a little more.
Charades are for us older folk;
Our flaws we can ignore.

But there is something age can't change;
It's always young and pure.
It is the soul God gave to us.
Forever we endure.

A POETIC THOUGHT

Within the coolness of the night
I watched a cotton-batten sky.
The drifting blanket clouds of mist
Caught the portal of my eye.

Then other issues held my mind
So I could not become the drift,
But I will keep the image close
Reminding me of spirit's lift.

BEGINNINGS

I watched the tiny leaves emerge
With all the pale soft of green.
Against a Wedgewood blue of sky
The new of life begins its gleam.

There's peeking buds and nasty gnats,
There's life in nests and water's flow.
Within the grass and in the air
The new of life is all aglow.

Long shadows on the meadow tell
Of towered trees and setting sun
Which gowns the green in golden hue,
A benediction. Day is done.

And then the sounds of twilight come
From life anew on Gaia's floor.
The peepers, crickets, tree frogs too
Announce their presence loud and more.

But I must not forget the blaze
Of blossoms grand in blooming bright
Where Cherry, Quince and Dogwood trees
Festoon the landscape's scenic sight.

There must be praise for what I see,
And to the Source my spirit goes
For there creation manifests
Into the poet's rambling prose.

The Milkweed Pod

I wonder when our lives are done,
If there is something past the Sun?
I feel it in a pod display
And see it in a light array.

The wings of down sustain the life
When seed pods burst in seeming strife.
There must be more beyond the pod
When usefulness becomes the sod.

The downy seeds will take their flight
Upon the breeze of day or night
And start anew in place supreme
To let their souls expand their dream.

Nature's Art

True nature has her time and look
If we but pause from busy's book.
We know it's not her time of cold,
Yet soon she'll make her presence bold.

Leaf's color now will set the space
For all of us to see and trace
The wonder of her art and craft
And knowing that it cannot last.

There is a canvas all around
On mountain peak and sandy sound.
So look within and find your art.
Then you and Nature will not part.

Old Warrior

I did my thing, the noble thing,
In battles of the past.
I think of that with metals pinned
Whose meaning didn't last.

There was a time when all were proud
And I would have a seat,
But youth today have other thoughts,
Their memory incomplete.

But when I pass and go beyond
The portal of the light,
I'll know the reasons for my life
And why I had to fight.

Night Storm

The joy of rain came passing through
My elemental sphere of life–
A type of storm, though known but new,
That set for some a passing strife.

With falling limbs from gust and strike
And tearing heaves of Nature's breath,
The flash and sound of lightning's might
Delayed by many miles of depth.

Each storm is like an Escher paint
Complete with knowing its return,
But I embrace with no complaint
The fury's force without concern.

MOON PINE

Oh, let me see below the pine
To where your heart is ever free.
Between the boughs and needled leaves
I see your light that's shared with me.

I am the Moon, a cratered orb,
That orbits Earth in cycled time,
Reminding all of humankind,
You are a song, a dappled rhyme.

The Spirit Road

Some roads are traveled less as I once read,
But in my youth I did not understand
That roads need not be paved to ride or tread.
An aging life will know that paths are grand.
Within life's choice of ways are trails too
To let us stand aside, bestride, or walk,
And trust the wonder that each step's a school
To learn the truth of life: to walk the talk.
There's wisdom there at every bend and turn
For us to choose a straight or curving way
That's trodden or traveled with less sojourn.
We hope our choice of path will not array
The thinking from within our outer mind
That leaves the spirit road so far behind.

THE LAKE

There is a place where family goes
Beyond the strife of daily clime,
To where the light and water glows
And mountains blend as if in rhyme.

There's history there of family ties
And memories of childhood,
When life and times had different sighs
And children played by shore and wood.

In time there came another home
On land adjacent to what's known,
In many ways a palindrome
Of what's before and what is sown.

New visions came from dreams and mind,
And crafters set them in its place
For family, friends, to all unwind
Where cares and troubles all erase.

Creation always has a name
Where thoughts and hopes are held keepsake.
The beauty wrought from place and frame
Does name the pristine home "The Lake."

But now the home does ache and weep.
It's missing one, a gentlemen.
He left to go to Heaven's sleep
Where we will be when we are done.

So what's to happen to this place
That holds a past from long ago?
No passage eases family's trace,
But how we wish he did not go.

Dedicated to the memory of Jay Andretta

A Metaphoric Boat

There! In the boat. My destiny.
My future cast afloat.
Dare I swim and try to see
What's in the auger boat?

The sea is me and I am bold
To stay within its brine.
My body's young, my spirit's old
And knows the path sublime.

Most do not know the Indigo
Are here to change–refine–
The way we stage our love tableau
Among our humankind.

That's all I know without the boat
To tell me what's in store.
The distance is Poseidon's moat
And keeps me near the shore.

It's deep and dark to brave the tide
And see my future clear,
So I will stay and play life's side
Despite the knowing near.

Unlike the boat that points her prow
To ocean swells unknown,
Again in life I'll live the NOW,
A choice that I have sown.

Village Green

It's snowing on the village green
Where drifts of white are clearly seen
And trees are lit with colors bright
For magic sleighs to see at night.

Small children play and run around
And toss the snow that's on the ground,
Their rosy cheeks and mittens white
Announcing soon it's Christmas night.

Some carolers stroll 'long the green
To sing the songs of season's scene
For it's a special time of year
Of goodwill hopes and Christmas cheer.

Yet sleighs and songs are symbols for
A lasting gift of time before,
Where birth and breath did crown a king
And angels taught the earth to sing.

But on the green the glee runs free
With children laughing round the tree.
They know not yet the gifts of God,
But time will change their mind's façade.

Perhaps their laughs and hopes are one
To hold all joy beyond the sun
Where sleighs and trees are metaphor
For peace on earth for evermore.

THE BELLS OF CHRISTMAS

The bells of Christmas sound their ring,
And call for all to be of cheer,
And share with those who choose to sing
The songs of joy from life's veneer.

Each bell reminds us, make a wish,
The same or different every year.
To hug and love all those we cherish,
And for the ones we shed a tear.

We're missing those who serve away,
And can't be home at Christmas time.
We thank them for their gifts forte
On land, in air, and maritime.

To all, I ask you on this night;
What is your wish this Christmas year?
Is it toys or perhaps a bike
Or just a cup of Christmas cheer?

SNOWBIRDS

Quilted coats, shuffled steps and canes
Are what you find on southbound trains.
The halt, the lame, the elderly
The ill, the weak, and crotchety
Are Florida bound in cubby holes
With all their flaws and hairy moles.

Snowbirds they're called without respect.
They flock to Florida's warmth prospect.
If you are younger and can watch,
Count the wrinkles, and see the blotch,
And you will know where you may be
Before they cite your eulogy.

SPRING THOUGHTS

It's Friday once again, you know,
Where weary workers choose to show
Four days of sweat and toiled tasks
Relaxing in night's freedom masks.

To bars and movies some will go
And others choose a Broadway show
And some of you will find a chair
To toss your worries in the air.

If you're retired, things do change.
Priorities may now seem strange
To those who need to work and toil
When all we need is new topsoil.

For me I know what I must do—
What all retirees find true.
Old autumn leaves need to be raked
And vines and flowers must be staked.

There're mowers, seeds and rows to start
Along with plants to set apart.
Some trims need paint and others nails
To keep a look for household sales.

I often think to let it go
But when it's nice, I do not know.
A house is more than something owned;
It is a home of love enthroned.

Where would I go if I left here?
The south or west? Not north I fear.
The east would put us in the sea
And then we surely would not be.

So let me talk 'bout warming spring
Where flowers bud and songbirds sing.
I love the fact it's Friday too
And winter's cold I've bid adieu.

The Potter's Clay

We are the potters of our clay,
We sculpt our images to time;
Despite some choices that delay,
It is our living paradigm.

Within the center of our soul
Is truth and love as light unfolds.
In there we find the chaliced bowl
That forms our clay in sacred molds.

It's different though from what we're taught—
To plant our life in dogma's creed.
Someday we'll wonder, in our thought,
If there is more to spirit's seed.

As in all things upon the earth,
Life is the way it ought to be.
We each create our pain and mirth;
It's choice that's hard when will is free.

So worry not with heavy mind
For people's choice you can't control.
It is the way of humankind
To learn the love that's in each soul.

THE PEPPER MILLS OF TRUTH

I had a vision in my dream
Or maybe it was just a thought,
But there I was upon a beam
Wondering if it would be caught

As it was sent down to below
To anyone who heard the tunes.
The image was to teach and show
And not be changed by casting runes.

The message was a simple thing:
There is no right, there is no wrong.
Just listen to the sacred ring
To know that all is all a song.

Rolland G. Smith has over fifty-five years of professional broadcast experience as an anchor, a reporter, producer and commentator. During his career he has been honored by the National Academy of Television Arts and Sciences with twenty-five Emmy nominations and has received eleven Emmy Awards. Highlights of his years in broadcasting include presidential interviews, front-line coverage of the Vietnam War, anchoring the international broadcast feed of "Live Aid" to an audience in excess of two billion, and being the first journalist to accompany the U.S. Geological Survey Team inside Mount St. Helens after the volcano's devastating eruption. Along with his extensive experience in broadcasting, Mr. Smith has an expressed interest in global issues, including the future of the environment (both physical and spiritual).

Highly sought after as a public speaker, he often includes in his engagements readings from his poetry, in which he uses the magic of rhyme as an avenue to communicate his viewpoint. His first book of poetry, *Quiet Musings*, was nationally released in August 1995 and was soon followed by his first CD, *Syl.la.bles*, which combines beautiful original music with his poetry readings. His two subsequent book releases were entitled *Encore: The Poetry of Nature* and *Stone Wisdom: Poems and Commentaries*.

Currently he is writing and producing independent documentaries and continues to write daily commentaries on his Internet blog at www.rollandgsmith.com.

www.ingramcontent.com/pod-product-compliance
Lightning Source LLC
Chambersburg PA
CBHW061537050726

47593CB00002B/812